Listening in the Shadows

Richard Thompson

Pen Press

First published in Great Britain in 2008
Pen Press is an Imprint of
Indepenpress Publishing Ltd
25 Eastern Place
Brighton, BN2 1GJ

ISBN 978-1-906710-44-6

Printed and bound in the UK by Cpod, Trowbridge, Wiltshire
A catalogue record of this book is available from the British Library

Cover design by Jacqueline Abromeit

For my loving wife, Janet.

Richard Thompson retired after 27 years police service in 2002 and fulfilled a lifelong ambition, to study and learn about the animal kingdom. He spent 3 years at Sparsholt College, Hampshire where he achieved a degree in animal science. Practical experiences were gained at various zoological establishments and a short time observing elephant behaviours in South Africa. After a spell at Longleat Safari Park he left to write about wildlife and pursue a passion for bat conservation.

Contents

Introduction

The name bat is derived from the Scandinavian word *bakke* and entered the English language in the late 16th century. This animal has to be one of the most unique creatures in the natural world, a mammal that flies with many species reliant on hearing for sight and the ability to suspend in an upside down position. One of the advantages of being nocturnal is the opportunity to avoid competition for suitable food resources that may not be accessible during the day. The ability to take advantage of the night skies is an evolutionary adaptation with successful results and this also means less competition and fewer predators. These flying mammals tend to have an enigma and a mystery being associated with the supernatural, dark secrets and nightmares. The spectral image of an aerial bat silhouetted against a full silvery moon lighting up the black sky and the distant twinkling stars is usually guaranteed to produce a cold shiver. This almost dreamlike vision is very vivid and perhaps the first picture conjured up in the mind.

Throughout evolutionary history bats have probably been one of the most successful of all the mammalian species. True flight evolved over many generations allowing what was believed to have been a small arboreal shrew like animal the opportunity to extend their range. As they adjusted to new and varied habitats, survival meant searching out a variety of food resources and to flourish, finding mates who were also equally successful. Today the 1000 or so known species are found on all the worlds continents except Antarctica and just about every niche and every habitat from tropical rain forest to arid deserts and parts of the Arctic Circle to areas with temperate climates. The numbers and diversity of species that have acclimatized and survive is one of natural histories most fascinating triumphs. In order to learn a little about the bat, it is necessary to go back through time and into evolutionary history. Fossil remains have been dated as far back as 50 to 60 million years suggesting that the ancestors may have been evolving towards the end of the dinosaur era. In recent years there has been considerable discussion on the origins of the fruit bats as they possess certain anatomical and physiological features that are significantly different and appropriate to an animal with contrasting survival strategies to the other species. Recent scientific conclusions favour that all bats share a more commonly related lineage and that they are rightfully placed together in the correct order. More accurately would be to state that there are two sub-orders.

Colonies of bats are often referred to as roosts or camps and the locations for these are nearly as diverse as is the numbers of species. Coping with extreme weather and avoiding predators will influence where roosts occur and the availability of food, which may also be seasonal is relevant and practical. From an ecological point of view the right environment for these animals to thrive is essential and literally means the difference between life and death. Over the years there has been a massive decline in bat numbers around the world, including the UK species. Some are more vulnerable than others and as with all wild animal species, bats are sensitive to disturbance and the ever increasing threat of habitat loss. Conservation efforts have and are proving effective but there is always work to be done and organisations such as the Bat Conservation Trust actively promote preservation by getting people involved and encouraging education. This book does not refer to every known species as the emphasis will generally be specifically about the UK species but includes comparisons with others from around the world. Hopefully this will give the reader an insight into this remarkable and extraordinary creature.

In concluding the introduction it would appear that the debate about the origins of the bat are more or less settled and that they all share a common ancestry with fruit bats. It could be however, that they may share a convergent evolution through many generations in which both groups of species evolved distinctive characteristics independently of each other and adapted to similar life strategies, circumstances, environments and habitats. This is one of the wonderful concepts of zoology and the natural world – we will never learn enough.

Evolution

About 200 million years ago during a geologic time period known as the Jurassic period early species of small secretive fur covered creatures existed alongside the then dominant land animals, the dinosaurs. At the end of the subsequent Cretaceous period some 135 million years later there was a massive extinction of many animals and in particular, the dinosaurs disappeared. The niche in the environment that this event left was soon filled by probably the most successful animals ever, the mammals. Amongst the survivors were the small insectivorous shrew like tree dwellers which through many evolutionary stages would develop into the bat. These ancestors were likely to have been a nocturnal prey species and one reason for their eventual success was the ability to maintain internal bodily temperatures which allowed them to be active and move about at night. This adeptness enabled the exploitation of a niche and food resources that were not readily available to other animals. The origins of these small mammals are believed to have started some 300 million years ago during the late Carboniferous. Descending from reptiles over a time scale of about 150 million years fur replaced scales and with many anatomical and physiological changes they were now becoming the dominant terrestrial animals. The Cretaceous was a very important time in evolutionary history with the influence and diversification of flowering plant species attracting insects and therefore providing food. Through natural selection the fittest survived and in time the bat ancestors gained the ability to glide. This was a tremendous adaptation which would have transformed not only survival but allowed an extended range and the opportunity to seek out better resources and mates. In time with the development of wing muscles powered flight has enabled the bat to be one of the most successful of all the mammals. Equally important during a time period spanning many millions of years between the Jurassic and Cretaceous was and still is a phenomenon called Continental Drift. This theory concerns the movement of the earth's land masses and in particular during the significant Cretaceous divided the 2 huge areas of land known as Laurasia and Gondwana. Laurasia became what at present is the northern hemisphere and Gondwana the southern. This obviously had some effect on the distribution of all animals and plant species and the eventual evolution of the bat. The fossil record is incomplete and it is estimated that more than half of the record is missing. It appears that there are many missing links in the evolutionay chain.

The earliest known bat remains have been dated to around 50 - 60 million years. Two of the oldest fossil bats are called *Icaronycteris* (I-caron-i-cer-teris) *index* and *Onychonycteris* (On-e-chon-e-cer-teris) *finneyi* and both were discovered in Wyoming, North America. The latter is believed to be the older of the two species and has certain characteristics that differ from the former, in particular the ear structure. The conclusion reached suggests that flight developed before echolocation, the opposite to what had previously been thought. This presumably means that as an insectivore, this bat must have had other ways of finding food. Learning more about evolution does appear to leave additional questions and many of the answers are still to be found. Today bats are divided into the 2 sub-orders, the megabats which are also called flying foxes and the microbats which are all the others that are not fruit bats. Considerable research during the 1980's suggested that fruit bats evolved later possibly separating from primates, that includes us. It is not certain, but all the available evidence indicates that each of the known bat species today is descended from a common ancestor and that the megabats branched from the microbats. The oldest megbat fossil has been dated around 23 – 38 million years and is known as *Archaeopteroptus* (Arch-e-op-ter-op-tus) *transiens*. Along with another fossil specimen found in Africa, that at present is about it. Interestingly there is evidence from about 70 million years ago to suggest that early moths had the ability to detect echolocating bat calls. This would indicate that bats had appeared a lot sooner than the evidence apparently suggests. From all the information and data currently available it is believed that all bats have descended from the original shrew-like animals and that they all followed the same evolutionary path. There is also the possibility that a sudden rise of around 7 degrees C in global temperatures about 50 million years ago had some influence as well. What is in doubt and perhaps always will be is the timing of the appearance of this fascinating and intriguing animal – the bat.

Bat fossil believed to be *Icaronycteris index*

Anatomy

It is necessary for the bat to remain light weight and this has been achieved by a rigid, yet light bone structure and thin wing membranes. The most obvious features are the elongated bones that make up the fore limbs or hand, known as metacarpal bones which provide support and enable wing manipulation. They have four fingers known as phalanges and an adjacent thumb which also has a useful claw for hanging in an upright position, often whilst urinating and defecating. The wing membrane extends along the body and in some species attaches to the hind limbs and the tail. When resting the wings can be folded like an umbrella and in doing so reduce heat loss or they can be flapped whilst panting and this helps to keep the animal cool in warm temperatures. The females also provide protection for their offspring, or pups by wrapping them inside their folded wings. The basic structure of the bat wing, or patagium is an adaptation of the mammalian limb and is a continuation of the bats body. Some species also have a tail membrane which when positioned downwards in flight assists in both the capture of insects and considerable manoeuvring abilities. The flexible wing membrane consists of two thin layers of skin and contains muscle, which controls the tension whilst flying, nerves and a supply of blood vessels. The power required to move the wings is supplied by additional muscles in the chest and back, making this the heaviest part of the body. They are exceptionally good flyers with cambered wings for manoeuvring at low speeds. The principle for flight is much the same as for birds, air flows faster over the upper surface of the wing because of its curved shape, so has slightly further to go. This results in low pressure above the wing and high pressure below, combined with the thrust of the powerful flight muscles to overcome the resistance of the air and the downstroke plus beating of the angled wings - lift is accomplished. It also seems that they can maintain power by turning and twisting the wings backwards during the upstroke which also helps to avoid air resistance. The advantage of a wing covered in skin enables sudden changes in direction, helpful in avoiding predators and if relatively minor damage is suffered will usually heal quickly.

Bat Wing

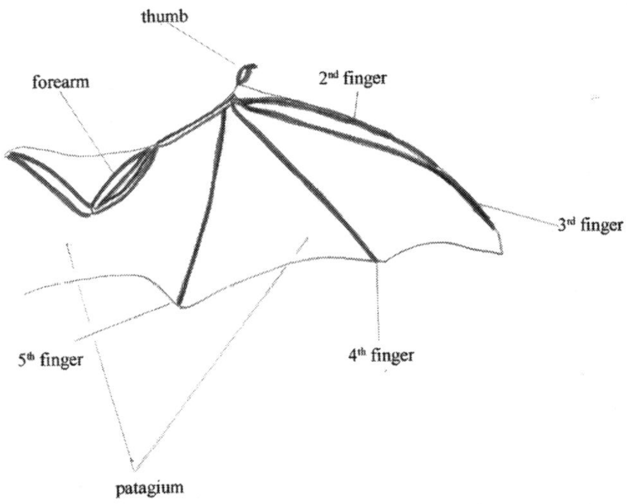

It is also worth mentioning that the energy required for flight is considerable and it is necessary for the heart rate to increase appreciably. From something like 300 beats per minute at rest to about 1000 beats per minute in the bat compared with 35 beats per minute and 70 beats per minute in elephants and humans respectively. Clearly in the case of bats it is vital that efficient energy conservation is both maintained and not wasted. The heart beats for a bat per minute during hibernation are around 20 – 25, although this may vary with species and ambient temperature.

Another unique feature, common to all bat species and especially useful to cave dwellers are legs with knees that face the opposite way to other mammals. This is because the hip joint is rotated 90 degrees and enables the bat to grip and use all four limbs to move speedily across a cave roof or other structure. When at rest they hang in an upside down position with sufficient height to drop and fly off. In order to hang safely they have evolved sharp claws on their lower limbs with which they can hook on to a relatively smooth surface by spreading them to gain a grip at different angles. The grip is maintained by leg tendons which when taut close the claws and keep them clenched and the bat can remain like this for several days. This is also assisted by the fact that the bats weight is greater than its skeleton, so in effect acts as a counterbalance. Some species such as the vampires have evolved strong leg muscles which enable them to literally run quite fast when targeting a prey animal. Another evolutionary achievement that has evolved is the ability to alter their bodily temperature, which should normally be somewhere between 30 and 35 degrees C, but whilst at rest this can be lowered to around 20 degrees C. This means that they can economize, within reason on the amount of food required to generate energy. One feature that is probably unequalled in the world of mammals is the ability to fly. This one aspect of evolution has made the bat an extraordinary and exceptionally successful species. This crucial and pivotal development has enabled these animals to open up and colonize many varied and diverse habitats and wing shape in particular has played an important role. For example some species such as the long eared bats will usually have broad but short wings, this provides the skill to get very close to vegetation and when appropriate to hover as they pick off insect prey. Other species have long narrow wings, so are more likely to be found in open spaces. True flight also gives bats the opportunity to cover a wider range in which to forage and this ties in with the impressive and very efficient echolocation. All bats and certain fruit bats within the *Rousettus* species can search for food and avoid obstructions in complete darkness. These ultrasonic sounds, or shouts bounce off solid objects and by analysis of the returning echo the bat can determine distance, direction and size as well as evading anything else that might be in the way, such as a building or trees. The ultrasonic sounds are known as pulses created in the larynx, or voice box and are well above our hearing, but from the bats point of view are very useful. The pulses are emitted in numerous short bursts and as the bat approaches prey or an obstacle or both, the shorter the time is for a returning echo. Therefore the pulses increase during the search phase from something like 12 per second to around 200 per second during the terminal phase. As the bat gets closer and with incredible accuracy, the bat receives what could be described as a sound picture of the immediate environment. Pulses work in frequencies, the length of which provides the required information and these will also vary with flight behaviours, foraging habitat and prey. The intensity of the frequency differs between species and there may even be differences between individuals within a species. Most species echolocate through the mouth but some, such as the horseshoe bats shout through the nose and this appears to direct the sound pulse in a particular direction. A higher rate of pulses provide a lot more information about the environment and improves the chances of catching prey safely. The retuning echo is picked up by a very sensitive ear structure and is transmitted along nerve impulses into the brain where the information is processed. But bats don't have it all their own way, there is a downside as pulses can be detected by potential predators and certain prey. Some moths for example have evolved complex ears and can listen for approaching bats. This obviously allows time for the insect to escape often by dropping to the ground and some species can emit a sound in response to confuse the bat. It maybe one of the reasons why some bat species fly quite low in an attempt to catch falling insects. Perhaps responding to other echolocating bats nearby. An interesting fact is that over time, reliance on echolocation may have reduced the need for vision, this being something that has apparently not affected most of the fruit bats, if they ever had this ability in the first place.

The one feature that always interests people is the bats ability to suspend upside down and remain in this position. The anatomy and physiology of all mammals is similar and the heart in particular is very important in this respect. This muscular organ controls the circulatory system and pumps de-oxygenated blood through arteries to the lungs. Gas exchange takes place where inspired oxygen is collected and carbon dioxide removed then expired. Veins return oxygenated blood back to the heart where valves prevent back flow and the blood is then pumped around the body where it diffuses. The bat cardiac cycle works in such a way that hanging upside down presents no problem, whereas all other known mammals and perhaps other creatures would soon find this harmful. Another advantage of this is that bats can literally drop into flight, providing they have allowed sufficient height and can escape predators.

Teeth are an important feature of the bat, those that are insectivorous obviously have small but sharp teeth and the jaws work in a scissor like way, chopping up their prey. The convenience of such small teeth is that there is no interference with the echolocating pulse calls. Fruit bats on the other hand rely on flat molar teeth to crush, grind and compress fruits. Also in common with all mammals, bats have a covering of usually dark and occasionally pale coloured fur and those found in the temperate climates need this protection as insulation against cold weather. There is, however the exception, some species are white, such as the Honduran white bat (*Ectophylla alba*) and other species may display various shades of orange, grey, yellow or amber, often stripped or patches or spots. This kind of colouration may also have something to do with camouflage and concealment, especially for those, such as roosting fruit bats that will be visible to predators in daylight. There is more variety in head or skull shape in bats than any other mammal and there appears to be a correlation between this and the appropriate food. For example some nectarivorous species from the Phyllostomidae (Plil-os-tom-e-day) family may have elongated muzzles for probing into flowers for nectar and others such as frugivorous fruit bats from the Pteropodidae (Per-terro-pod-e-day) family might have a broad face for biting into fruits. These species are also important pollinators inadvertently taking pollen from one plant to another.

In the 18th century a Swedish scientist called Carl Linnaeus created a system of classification for all animal and plant species using a specific Latin name for each. Today this subject is known as taxonomy and is the same for bats as well as any other animal. Every taxonomic name has to be original and unique and will identify that individual species. For example the common pipistrelle, a familiar UK species has been grouped within a genus known as Pipistrellus. Similar genera are placed in a family, in this example Vespertilionidae (Ves-per-ti-lion-e-day) and similar families are placed within an order, Chiroptera (Ki-rop-tera), then class, Mammalia and so on. The individual species name will always establish that particular animal, as many have more than one common name. The species name may refer to a person or a location and occasionally a description. For example there is a bat from the genus known as *Myotis* whose name means mouse eared bat with big feet, very original. Convention dictates that the genus and species names are always italicized with the others being shown in bold.

Kingdom	Animalia : all animals
Phylum	Chordata : animals with a backbone
Class	Mammalia : warm blooded animals that suckle young
Order	Chiroptera : meaning hand wing
Sub-Order	Megachiroptera (fruit bats) :
	Microchiroptera (bats that are not fruit bats)
Family	(example) : Vespertilionidae – in total 18 families
Genus	(example) : Pipistrellus
Species	(example) : pipistrellus

In the UK we have 16 species grouped in 2 families, the Rhinolophidae (Rhino-lop-he-day) with approximately 64 known species worldwide and the largest, of about 350 or so known species worldwide, the Vespertilionidae, or Vespers. The first family has two species within the same genus, the horseshoe bats and the remaining 14 species are placed in six genera. There is another species that has been recorded in the UK and is known as the mouse eared bat, but sadly there have been very few sightings in recent years.

Behaviours

Bats are without doubt one of the most social of all mammals, this basically means that individuals from the same species will cooperate when performing certain activities. This has both advantages and benefits in predator avoidance and locating foraging sites. There are however downsides such as competition for mates and the potential for disease. Natural selection appears to have helped bats to develop strategies that must outweigh or at least compensate for the costs and prosper from the benefits. Being one of a huge colony in an inaccessible roost is a good way of protection from the weather and the possibility of predation. There may even be an evolutionary connection with the wing structure folding neatly like an umbrella, so microbats can climb into very small crevices. Life for fruit bats is slightly different as most species roost in tree foliage especially the females, quite often males remain solitary or in small groups. That is until its time to create and maintain a territory with which to encourage the females. One of the most efficient ways of attracting females is to make good use of scent glands, called gular glands. With some species these are located around the throat, with others they have similar glands across the shoulders and yet others produce a delightful scent from the genital area. Its difficult to understand how this might work when mixed with urine and saliva, but it appears to be irresistible. Another seductive strategy that also apparently works is the production of a scent from bacteria in the arm pit. There are several other behaviours that are equally important such as vocalisation and the creation of leks. An example of which is the African hammer headed bat *Hypsignathus monstrosus* where anything up to 100 males will usually gather alongside or in the vicinity of a river. They will all suspend from adjacent vegetation and start to flap wings and produce deep amplified honking sounds. Females approach the line-out and after a quick inspection select those that are making the most noise. However, as this subject is so diverse we will stick with the example of the common pipistrelle, as this is a bat most people can relate to. The smallest known European bat, this is the most likely of the UK species to be seen flying fast at dusk during summer and autumn evenings. Generally they are the first to appear and their erratic flight distinguishes them clearly, often reaching a flight speed of around 22kph (14mph). They can be found in a variety of habitats, including domestic gardens, farmland, mature woodland and water. Usually at a height of about 6 metres (19.6 ft) these 8g (0.28 oz) nocturnal mammals exploit their night time niche searching for food resources – flying insects. Typical prey includes midges, mosquitoes and small moths and individual pips can munch their way through anything between an incredible 2,000 – 3,000 insects in one night. They are active from March to October and will spend most of the night foraging, however during May and June individuals often return to their roosts between midnight and dawn. This pattern changes later in the summer to intermittent feeding with peaks around sunset and dawn. The weather also plays an important part, many bat species seem able to detect changes, which is very useful in deciding whether using up energy to search for food, which may not be available is worth it.

The 43 or so known species of pipistrelle belong to the Vespertilionidae family and are found throughout most of the world except South America and the Antarctic. Their range also extends to parts of the Arctic Circle and some surprisingly northerly latitudes. Here in the UK we have 3 species, the common and the soprano which are relatively widespread and the extremely rare nathusius.

Mating will occur in the autumn but fertilisation (see reproductive behaviours) will not take place until the spring and following hibernation. Female pipistrelles are often mature by their first autumn and certainly within 2 years, when they will swarm at small maternity colonies where single pups are born after 40 to 50 days gestation

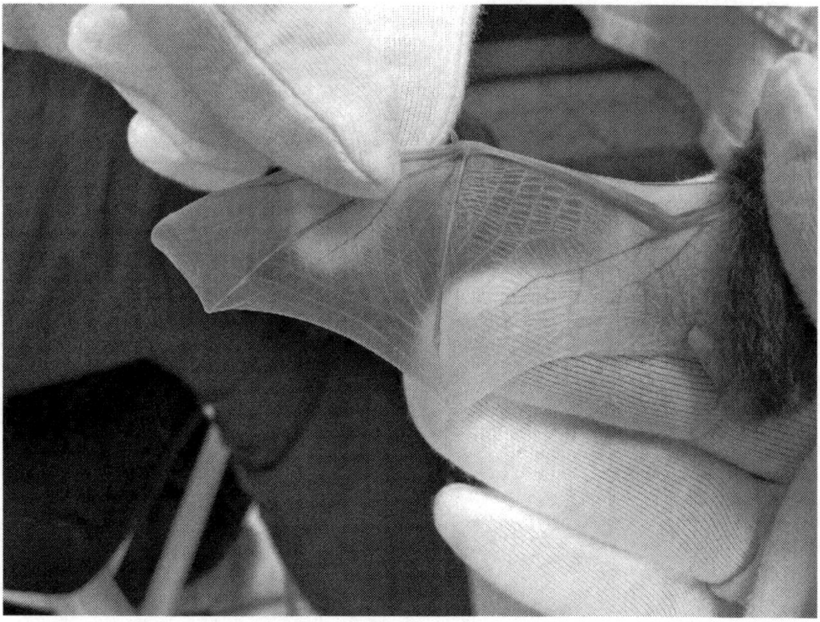

Semi-albino soprano pipistrelle wing

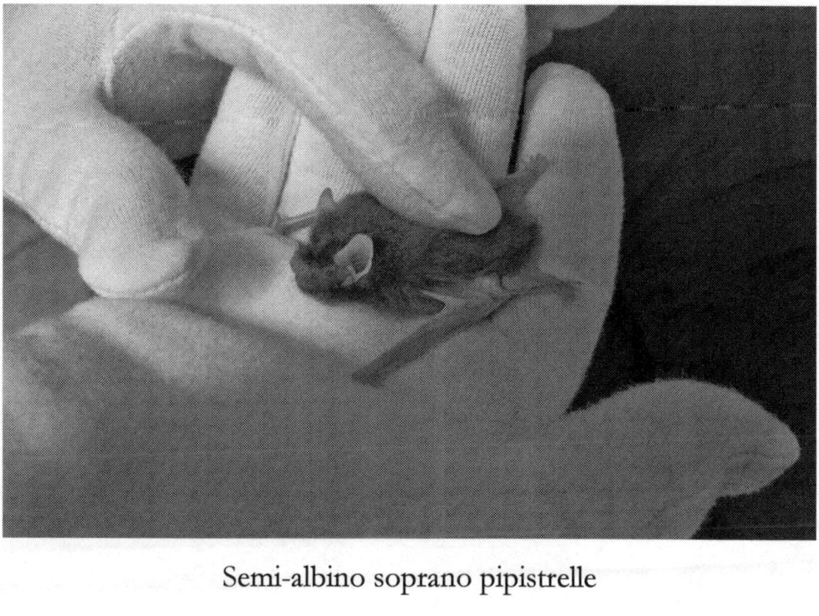

Semi-albino soprano pipistrelle

Common Pipistrelle

Pipistrelle statistics

Description	Colouration	Dark brown (appears black)
	Forearm	28 - 35mm
	Length	35 - 45mm
	Weight	6 - 8g
	Wingspan	190 - 250mm
Roost	Summer	Buildings - trees
	Winter	Buildings
Food resources	Spring – summer – autumn	Flies – midges – mosquitoes – small moths
Cycle	Mating	Autumn
	Maternity colonies	Spring-single pup born June/ July-weaned 6 weeks
	Life span	Up to 16 years

and are weaned by 6 weeks. In contrast most female fruit bats will always be at least around 2 years of age. During this time the roost is likely to be housing or other similar structures and occasionally they will move from one location to another. This is one reason why people who are aware of a roost behind, for example tiles or eaves wonder why they seem to have disappeared. Its quite amazing that a pipistrelle can access a hole or crack 13mm wide – that is about half an inch. Several summer roosts will be located within their individual territories and used to rest during night time foraging. Around mid summer they will also occasionally fly in daylight. They may also move roost if heavy predation (birds of prey and cats) occurs or any other disturbance or to follow food resources. Winter roosts are established by October or November in a variety of locations such as buildings, trees and bat boxes, they rarely enter caves or tunnels and again may change location from time to time i.e. very cold weather. They will also feed during spells of warm weather but are rarely seen until they emerge again the following April or May.

There is a wide variation in breeding strategies, generally the larger the bat the longer the gestation, which may also affect the time as well, for example lower temperatures mean slightly longer gestation. The female can in effect slow down pregnancy by entering a state of torpidity or dormancy if climatic conditions are not right or there is a lack of food and as a last resort the young may be abandoned. Many if not most males, including pipistrelles practice polygyny, which means 'many female', so the mating systems have evolved depending on certain conditions, such as environment, habitat and food. This system of polygamy works well for a dominant male individual with a suitable and well defended territory and where the male need not contribute any effort in bringing up offspring.

Dependent young soon bond with the mother who will usually give birth high in the roost and in the upside down position. The umbilical cord acts as a kind of safety rope and instinctively the pup makes for the nearest nipple. Females then often consume the placenta and afterbirth as this helps to bring on lactation. The 2g (0.07 oz) pup and mother can recognise each other very quickly through smell and

House roost access points

sound. Two features that distinguish the female bat in particular as a mammal are the abilities to both nourish and sustain young pups by the placenta in which a developing fetus receives nutrients, such as oxygen and the removal of wastes. The other is the provision of nourishing rich milk given by the mother between feeding activities during the night. This is vital and the female pipistrelles must consume about half their body weight every night during lactation. It is also important that they do not burn up energy unnecessarily so flying may be within a radius of 3 – 5km (less than 3 miles). Twins are very rare as the energy demands required would be extreme and many female species will also carry the pup for several weeks adding to a considerable burden.

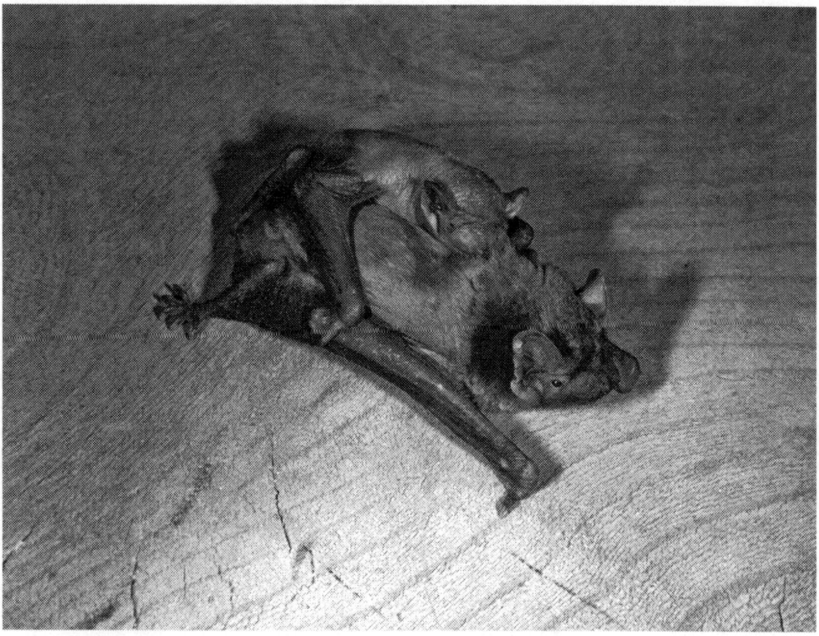

Noctule carrying Juvenile

Hibernation

Following the example of the pipistrelle again and all the species that have to respond to an absence of insect food. This tactic is also known as diapause and involves the bat entering a state of torpor, which is a very deep sleep and generally lasts for the duration of the winter. Many species have the option to migrate, but here in the temperate UK all bats have to store up on energy or fat to survive. Once a suitable site has been located the colony or occasionally a solitary individual will allow their body temperature to drop to around that of the ambient surroundings and the whole metabolic rate including the heart rate slows down. A typical temperature may be around 5 or 10 degrees C and it is also crucial that there is a reasonable amount of humidity as bats can dehydrate during hibernation. They might fly on warm winter evenings or nights, but this is risky if they burn up too much energy and then return to a dormant state, they may not survive. This brings about an interesting point in that there appears to have been an assumption that mortality was high after hibernation. Recent research suggests that there is no significant increase in loss of life and that more pipistrelles and presumably other species survive than had been previously believed. This remarkable animal can survive in this state by breathing about 5 times every 45 minutes or so or even longer in order to save energy. In order to do this the bat must feed well before the onslaught of winter so as to build enough fat reserves. This is sometimes difficult for the female if she has been unable to store sufficient fat due to the efforts of bringing up young during the summer. There are also occasions when the bats body temperature will increase slightly by about a couple of degrees, allowing the metabolism to return to normal. This then generates the opportunity for bursts of activity to find food or water, but this will use up a lot of stored energy, which could prove costly later. Another problem with hibernation is if a colony or individual is disturbed and they start flying or come out of torpor they can starve as a considerable amount of energy will be used. Once used it cannot be utilised again and is lost, meaning that the bat may not have enough in reserve to survive. It has to be remembered that bats are relatively defenceless with wings instead of arms and legs that are holding the animal in place, so the hibernation site needs to be safe. If a bat is disturbed it will take at least half an hour to reach a state of alertness, leaving the animal vulnerable.

Tunnel hibernation site

Union Canal

Feeding behaviours

The vast majority of bats feed on insects but there are some that specialise in a resource that is not always associated with these animals, fish. Clearly every bat has a particular style of foraging in specific habitats, such as woods, the use of echolocation and wing shape. Insects that are taken in flight is known as hawking, others are gleaned from the ground or vegetation or by gaffing from surface water. Prey can be caught by the mouth or scooped up in the wings. An example of the unique fishing skills are demonstrated by one of two species from a family known as Noctilionidae (Noc-ti-lion-e-day). These bats have several common names but are often called the fishing bats and are found in central and northern South America always near water, including the sea. They have evolved the ability to echolocate shoals of fish by detecting ripples on the surface. The bat then flies and glides in a zigzag pattern slowly just above the surface and drops its claws below, trawling for several metres attempting to impale prey up to 10cm (3.9ins) long. Once captured the bat will often chew on the fish and place small chunks in cheek pouches and continue fishing or will fly to a perch for consumption. Two amazing facts about this bat are firstly if there is the possibility of a collision with another bat, they will call out loud honking sounds as a warning. The other is if one falls into the water they can swim and have been known to use their wings as oars plus an additional ability to take off from the water. These bats are generally nocturnal but they have been observed in the daytime fishing in company with pelicans. There seems little doubt that every known species of bat has evolved varied nocturnal feeding behaviours. Through adaptation they have the ability to endure and survive in a variety of climates and conditions. It is very likely that by being active in the darkness they avoid direct competition from birds and are less vulnerable to predators. This raises an interesting question about the species that live in the extremes of the Arctic Circle, such as the northern bat, a relative of the serotine, where at certain times of the year they are exposed to constant daylight. Research suggests that part of the answer may be to do with the lowest levels of light which occur between 10pm and 2am. This could perhaps mean that fewer birds of prey are hunting during these hours. It might also mean that this species, for example still maintains some evolutionary nocturnal behaviours.

Bat families

There are many reasons why bats are misunderstood and as many quotations that are equally wrong, the classic being blind as a bat. Belfries would be far too cold and draughty and probably noisy. The one fact that has given the bat a bad name is the association with the Dracula novels and throughout history people have always feared what they do not understand. Ironically in Chinese culture the bat represents five blessings, long life, wealth, health, virtue and a natural death. In many other cultures there are folk tales and stories from the ancient Greeks. Bats are very intelligent and clean and as part of a social society grooming plays an important part in daily life. They help to prevent the spread of disease by insects and are integral in sustaining many worldwide ecosystem.

The largest bats, or megabats are those that live off fruits and they get referred to as flying foxes due to their size and in particular their colouring and facial features. There are something like 170 or so known species of which all are more or less the same shape, but vary considerably in size depending on species. Their range is extensive from Africa through much of southern Asia, Indonesia and Australia. We will concentrate on one typical example, which also happens to be my favourite, the Egyptian fruit bat *Rousettus aegyptiacus*. This species is found in the lowlands and mountains of the Mediterranean Middle East and throughout sub-Saharan Africa. One of the reasons for the conflict over ancestry is that the fossil evidence starts at 38 million years ago, suggesting a later evolution than all the other known species. From the information that is available it would appear that all bats branched out from the shrew-like mammal. However it is possible that the fruit bats may have diverged independently and had been more squirrel-like in appearance. In any event the fruit bats also had to avoid predators, find food resources and search for mates. Over time and many generations they evolved through natural selection which allowed the fittest to survive and adapt to new and varied habitats. This particular fruit bat was discovered in the early 19th century roosting in the pyramids at Giza in Egypt by a French naturalist called Etienne Geoffroy Sanit-Hilare (1772 – 1844). This was an appropriate location and typical habitat as they will often congregate in large numbers in dry humid sites, caves are particularly good examples. It is now known that their staple diet is wild and occasionally cultivated fruits, which of course brings them into conflict with people and sadly this means that in some countries they are considered pests and subject to control. Ironically there is evidence suggesting that fruit bats and this species in particular only feed on ripened yields which are of no or little use to humans. The Egyptian fruit bat is placed in the genus *Rousettus* and consists of the only group of these bats that echolocate. This may have something to do with the fact that they dwell in the dark areas of caves, where even good eyesight is not sufficient. Although good flyers they appear to lack some of the aerial skills perfected by others but they do have powerful jaws and prominent teeth for crushing tough fruit skins. An occasional feeding treat is the sweet tasting nectar of flowering plants, which also means that they inadvertently collect and distribute pollen spores. This is one of the smallest of the fruit bats with a body length around 15cm (5.9 ins), a wingspan of some 60cm (1.9 ft) and weighing in at 130-150g (4.5-5.2 oz). It is quite common for them to cover a large range in the search for food, including day time activities despite an increase in the risk of predation by birds of prey. Why the echolocating ability is restricted is not known, it may be that other fruit bats did have the capability and that it was lost through lack of use, if they ever had it in the first place. The Egyptian fruit bats use echolocation purely for navigation and this is achieved by rapidly clicking the tongue in order to generate the pulse. They do this by flicking the tongue up and as one edge lifts before the other, there is a slight time delay. This creates two signals, the second being about 30ms after the first. The time delay between the pulse and the intensity of the reflected echo being picked up by the ears create a sound picture of their surroundings. The bat can see by listening in the shadows. Part of the answer as to why these individuals echolocate is that they will be located in the darkest area of a cave, old mine workings or similar habitat and this will help them to judge distances, avoid obstructions, such as each other or the cave walls and select the correct direction instantly.

Reproduction is not dissimilar to all the many other species of bats, but one fact does stand out, fruit bats do not hibernate. The Egyptian fruit bat females reach sexual maturity between 5 and 9 months and the males at about 15 months of age. In the wild reproductive cycles may be continuous with births usually in the spring and autumn. All female bats have to carry a developing fetus within their bodies and the female Egyptian fruit bat is no different. She will gestate for 4 months and usually one pup is born, which she has to carry for the first few weeks, so it is not surprising that twins are rare. Pregnancy will often coinside with low rain fall enabling lactation during the highest rainfall, so the fruit necessary to the diet will be at its best nutritional value. It is believed that breeding is timed with good food resources, even if that means travelling further in search of food. There is a also the strategy which enables a delay in implantation, if for example those food resources are limited. To give birth the mother will usually remain in the normal upside down roosting position with her wings held out. The pup will appear head first and followed by the wings and legs. This should only take a few minutes and the 22g (0.77 oz) pup may be suspended by the umbilical cord before climbing up on to the mothers abdomen, finding a teat under her wing and taking a drink of the rich milk. Any afterbirth is quickly consumed by the mother. This is when bonding takes place with the very important activity of grooming and chirping. In a roost that may contain hundreds if not thousands of pups it is vital that each mother can identify her own offspring. This is believed to be achieved by both the chirping communication and the act of grooming that leaves a distinctive scent. After 6 weeks the weaned pup is able to fly and will remain with the colony, or camp. The slightly larger males do not appear to have an active part in rearing the infants and their reproductive strategy is polygyny, (many female). This means that in this particular group of social animals there is a lot of competition between the males to pass on their genes to the next generation.

It is quite common for these animals to go into a daily torpor whilst at rest, this seems to last for several hours at a time and occasionally all day long. This is an efficient way of saving energy by slowing down the metabolism. Another feature that distinguishes them from other fruit bats is the fact that they choose to roost in caves or mines or other similar structures and not trees or shrubs. Using their good eyesight in searching for and locating fruits and with their keen sense of smell, they will spend some time circling the vicinity, perhaps checking for a predator ambush before feasting. They will take the juicy fleshy part and often spit out seeds and sometimes fill their cheek pouches to take food away, somewhere safer and quiet. All mammals need to control their natural bodily processes and there is evidence to suggest that bat behaviours have evolved around a 24 hours long cycle known as the circadian rhythm, Latin for 'approximate day'. This relates mainly to the recurrent series of biological events and variations required for survival, such as body temperature and metabolism. These conditions have to be synchronised with the environment and habitat that the animal finds itself in. For example this species will be mainly active at night and feeding may be timed to avoid increasing levels of light at around dawn, the distance the bat has to return to the roost and the potential for aerial predator attacks. In the wild and to some extent in captivity, roosting behaviours will be influenced by social structure, food resources, mating and predator avoidance. In the wild an Egyptian fruit bat might live for between 8 and 10 years and in captivity up to 20 or even 30 years. Another interesting fact is that this species has been found in colonies consisting of some 3,000 individuals, one of the largest animal groupings in the world today. In such gatherings males, females and juveniles will be tightly packed together, very important for an animal living in a gregarious community. Potentially dangerous to the species if such large groups were to be exterminated on a regular basis, but at present the Egyptian fruit bat is not endangered and it is clear that with climate change and continuous habitat loss their range will increase north into southern Europe eventually.

UK and other species

The table below names the species with their respective Latin names, status, typical examples of food and general area of the UK where they will be found. All these species use the ultrasonic echolocating calls, or pulses. By listening to the reflected sound waves they navigate and find insect prey in the night time skies. The pulses produced will all vary depending on which activity and the immediate surroundings. The individual pulses can be identified but this does need a lot of time and patience and a bat detector. As we are unable to hear the sounds these devices convert the original call to something that we can hear. These clicks, tocks, smacks, slaps and warbles are the most amazing sounds and with experience individual species frequencies can be established. There are many detectors available and not all are expensive, possibly the best way to start is to use the heterodyne system. Most bats sweep through 45kHz and by tuning the dial up and down to the deepest pitch and noting the call at its peak will help identify the bat. You will also have to consider other facts such as location in the UK, habitat and flight pattern, is it erratic, fast or slow, diving or straight perhaps hovering and rarity. Today it is quite easy to find out a wealth of information about these animals and the work of conservationists.

Barbastelle	*Barbastella barbastellus*	Rare	insects-moths-spiders	England and South Wales
Bechstein	*Myotis bechstenii*	Rare	beetles-mosquitoes-moths	Central and Southern England
Brandts	*Myotis brandtii*	Rare	insects-moths-spiders	England and Wales
Brown long eared	*Plecotus auritus*	Common	beetles-moths-spiders	Throughout UK
Daubentons	*Myotis daubentonii*	Common	caddisflies-mayflies-midges	Throughout UK
Grey long eared	*Plecotus austriacus*	Rare	beetles-moths	Central and Southern England
Greater horseshoe	*Rhinolophus ferrumequinum*	Rare	beetles-chafers-craneflies-moths	SW England and South Wales
Leislers	*Nyctalus leisleri*	Rare	beetles-caddisflies-moths	Throughout UK to S.Scotland–not Wales
Lesser horseshoe	*Rhinolophus hipposideros*	Rare	beetles-addisflies-lacewings-spiders	SW England and Wales
Nathusius (pip)	*Pipistrellus nathusii*	Rare	midges-mayflies-mosquitoes-moths	Throughout UK
Natterers	*Myotis nattereri*	Common	insects-moths-spiders	Throughout UK
Noctule	*Nyctalus noctula*	Common	beetles-mayflies-winged ants	Throughout UK to south Scotland
Pipistrelle	*Pipistrellus pipistrellus*	Common	midges-mayflies-mosquitoes-moths	Throughout UK
Soprano (pip)	*Pipistrellus pygmaeus*	Common	midges-mayflies-mosquitoes-moths	Throughout UK
Serotine	*Eptesicus serotinus*	Common	beetles-chafers-moths	S England and S Wales
Whiskered	*Myotis mystacinus*	Rare	insects-moths-spiders	Throughout UK and S Scotland

The largest of the UK bats are the noctules, the name of which dates from the 18th century and means night. Their range includes pastures, woodland edges and urban areas throughout England, Wales and southern Scotland, but not Ireland. This species is sadly in decline and it it believed to be down to the loss of feeding habitat and good roosting opportunities. This bat is usually one of the first to appear at dusk, often just before sunset. They have a narrow and pointed wing structure and their flight behaviour includes the ability to dive after insects from some height and reach a speed of 50kph (30mph). Most prey is caught and consumed whilst flying and a noctule may fly 10km (6 miles) from a roost to a foraging area. They are also known to take prey from the ground and will change their diet from midges for example in the spring to larger quarry during summer such as moths. During the summer months the males are generally solitary or associate in small bachelor groups. To attract the slightly larger females an individual will establish a tree roost and will call out to any passing by and with the assistance of an odour, will gather up a small harem, who remain together for a day or two. Fertilisation is delayed until spring as the female stores sperm inside the uterus during hibernation. Roosting and small maternity colonies are nearly always in natural tree holes, or those made by woodpeckers. During the spring they may also form up in mixed sex groups occasionally in buildings and very often in bat boxes, where they will sit on top of each other. Once the young are born and sometimes there are twins they suckle for about 4 weeks until weaned and can forage themselves at about 6 weeks. Again typical behaviour is to move from one roost to another with the pups being carried during lactation. When the females need to feed the young are left in a nursery, which again is typical of many bats. An occurrence that could have inadvertently helped noctules is the reduction in the numbers of starlings, who have been known to attack and kill them.

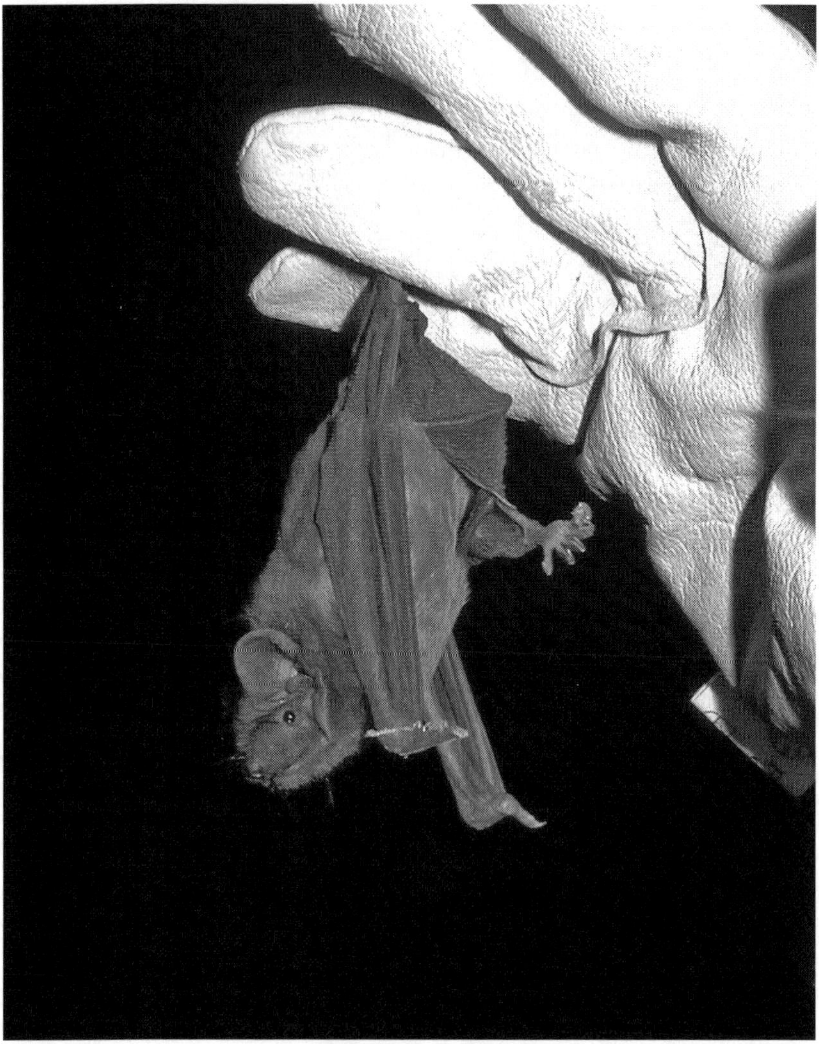

Noctule hanging

Nocutle statistics

Description	Colouration	Dark golden/brown
	Forearm	48 - 58mm
	Length	60 - 80mm
	Weight	18 - 40g
	Wingspan	320 - 400mm
Roost	Summer	Trees
	Winter	Trees – bat boxes
Food resources	Spring-summer -autumn	Midges – moths – beetles – winged ants
Cycle	Mating	Summer and autumn
	Maternity colonies	Spring – single/twins – weaned 4 – 6 weeks
	Life span	Up to 12 - 16 years

Other bat statistics

Name	Weight g	Wingspan mm	Summer roost	Winter roost	Typical habitat
Barbastelle	6 -13	245 - 290	buildings/ trees	trees/ cellars	woods/ water
Bechstein	7 - 13	250 - 300	trees	caves/ tunnels	woods/ farms
Brandts	5 - 9	210 - 255	buildings/ trees	caves/ tunnels	woods/ water
Brown long ear	6 - 12	230 - 285	barns/ churches	caves/ buildings	woods/ parks
Daubentons	7 - 12	240 - 275	bridges/trees	caves/ tunnels	woods/ water
Grey long ear	7 - 14	230 - 285	barns/ churches	caves/ tunnels	meadows
Gtr horseshoe	17 -34	350 - 400	buildings	cellars/ tunnels	woods/ water
Leislers	12 -20	260 - 320	buildings/ trees	buildings/ trees	woods/ parks
Les horseshoe	5 - 9	200 -250	roofs/stables	cellars/ tunnels	woods/ wetland
Nathusius pip	6 - 15	220 - 250	buildings/ trees	buildings	woodland
Natterers	7 - 12	245 - 300	buildings/ trees	caves/ tunnels	woods/ water
Soprano	3 - 8	192 -232	buildings/ trees	buildings	woods/ gardens
Serotine	15 - 35	320 - 380	buildings	buildings	woods/ gardens
Whiskered	5 - 9	190 - 250	buildings/ trees	caves/ tunnels	woods/ water

This is a very basic descriptive guide but gives an indication of the similarities and differences that all the UK species share. The advantages of flight also mean that these animals can move from one area to another and occasionally an individual(s) will turn up in the most unlikely place. Bats are divided up into 18 families, the largest being the vespers and a curious tiny bat known as Kitti's hog nosed bat, or bumblebee bat (*Craseonycteris thonglongyai*) is placed in its own family Craseonycteridae (Cras-sony-ser-teri-day). This diminutive 2g (0.07oz) bat has a 16cm (6ins) wingspan and pig-like muzzle is only found in the vicinity of the River Kwai in Thailand and an area of Myanmar. This tiny bat is also believed to be the smallest known mammal in the world. Ranging through bamboo forest and woodland they roost in limestone caves, but sadly are under immense threat as a result of habitat loss such as logging and are seriously endangered. In common with most other bats the few remaining animals hunt insect prey by echolocating or gleaning from vegetation.

Here in the UK the noctule, usually solitary is the largest of our indigenous bats and is very distinctive in the dusky summer skies, diving and abruptly changing direction. In contrast with our smallest, the common and soprano pipistrelles, which can be seen individually or in small groups flying in their own fast and characteristic, but erratic way. A bat flying very close to the surface of fresh water, such as a river or pond is very likely to be a daubentons. These bats will take insect prey just above and on the surface and have been known to use their tails as a scoop, possibly another adaptation for survival. Once it gets going a daubentons can reach speeds of up to 25kph (15mph) and may cover 6km (3.7miles) or more - not bad for a small mammal. Leislers bat is not unlike the noctule in appearance but with longer fur and a golden tint. This is quite a common bat, except in Scotland. These bats have been observed flying at tree top height, occasionally with a dive or two and also close to the ground. Leislers in urban areas will chase insects in the vicinity of street lighting. Grey long eared bats are confined to southern England but the brown long eared is very common throughout the UK. These appealing little bats have been reported roosting on oil rigs in the North Sea, suggesting that they, along with pipistrelles and noctules could be migratory. The ears of

Brown long-eared

both long eared species are almost as big as the individual carrying them, they really appear to be out of proportion, but are used to great advantage. Inside or on the edge of woodland, a brown will almost hover gleaning insects from vegetation. They might also glide or go into a steep dive and sometimes land to find prey. Greys generally take prey by hawking, or in flight and both may use nearby perches such as a field barn for larger insects. The natterers bat is named after an Austrian naturalist and is one of the few species to be found in Scotland. Although relatively common it is a significantly important bat in the UK because of habitat loss through timber treatment, particularly to older buildings. With broad wings they are capable of flying at slow speeds through woodland and alongside hedgerows and will also take insect prey to a perch. The serotine is similar in size to the noctule and is generally found from East Anglia to the West Country and South Wales. Flying at about tree top height within a few kilometres of their roosts, in a relaxed kind of way with broad wings flapping and the occasional glide, seemingly without a care in the world. They will also drop onto the ground or vegetation with outstretched wings to catch insects. Unfortunately and in common with some of the other species, the loss of habitat and suitable buildings for roosts is possibly causing serotine numbers to dwindle.

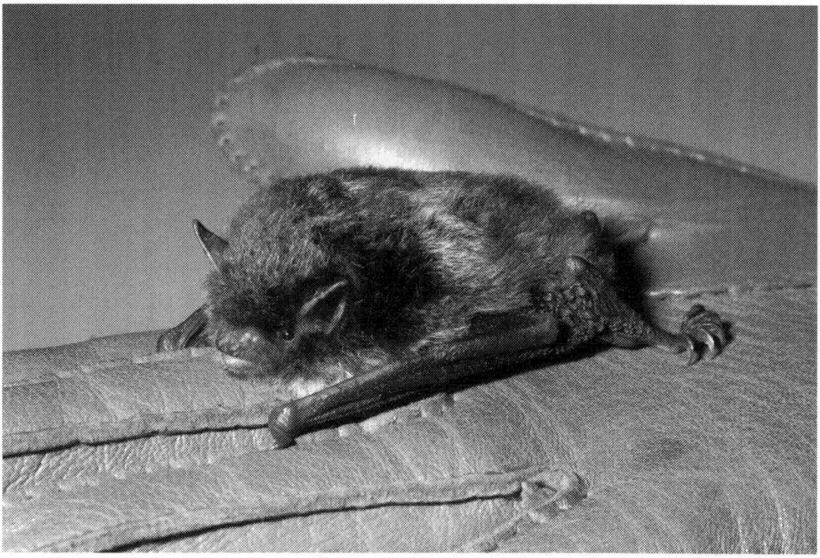

Daubenton's bat

Daubenton's bat habitat

Barbastelle

Bechstein's bat

Whiskered and brandts bats are very much alike and it takes some experience to identify one from the other. Both are thought to be active nearly all night long. Whiskered bats which are also found in southern Scotland and parts of Ireland have a fast fluttering flight behaviour and will swoop from a height of some 6 metres (19.6ft). They are also known to tend to stick to a particular route, such as a hedgerow. The brandts bat is generally more common and has a hasty and skilful flight pattern in woodland. Again, these two species are vulnerable to the destruction of habitat and particularly sensitive to pesticides. The name barbastelle means short beard which is where this bat gets its name as the muzzle is covered in stubble like hair. They were once described to me as flying gremlins, almost black in colour and with ears that join on the top of the head. This species is also very rare and are found only in the lower half of England and Wales. They are particularly sensitive to disturbance and insecticides plus the loss of old woodlands, means there is a serious risk of decline. They fly fast and low hawking prey in flight and their range will usually include enclosed woodland and an area of fresh water. Spring and summer roosting is often under tree bark and in the winter they will hibernate in hollow trees or in underground sites such as cellars. Another extremely rare and vulnerable bat is the bechstein found in the West country and east across to Sussex. This small bat is distinctly pale brown with a dark pinkish coloured face and long ears. In the summer the males are solitary and the female and juveniles may congregate in maternity roosts of 30 or more individuals.

There are a variety of survival strategies utilized by bats and how long they live depends on so many varied situations. Some species have been recorded aged over 20 years but in reality its probably much less, perhaps 4 to 6 or so years. Males are often difficult to tell apart from females without some practical handling experience. From remote dark forests to the urban street lights of towns and cities all the UK species will have to adapt to the apparent on-going climate change. Even at present the weather conditions of a temperate region with heavy rain and high winds are not popular with bats. Will any significant changes in climate affect bats, this is a subject with little known research to date. One fact that has been documented is the movement towards the north west of 2 species of pipistrelle, savi's from Africa and Asia and kuhl's from across Asia and as far away as Mongolia and Japan. Considerable change may alter many behaviours, such as hibernation, reproductive cycles and changes in feeding behaviours because of a lack or loss or change of prey. Some species might benefit, some will not, but then there may be no difference at all.

The largest known species of bat is a flying fox from the same family as the Egyptian fruit bats. It has several common names but is generally called the Malayan or large flying fox. This bat has a fearful sounding Latin name, *Pteropus vampyrus* but they are not related to the vampires. These black coloured bats are found in the Far East, in places such as Borneo and the Philippines often roosting in forest fig trees or mangroves. This bat has been recorded in camps of several hundred individuals or, rarely in their thousands. They are not presently endangered but as a result of hunting by humans for meat and pest control there is the risk of a decline. This is a big bat weighing around 1000g or two and a half pounds with a wingspan of 1.8 metres or six feet. It is not unusual for foraging expeditions to cover up to 60km (37miles) per night, although its not known if this is because of necessity or persecution. Typical diet consists of fruits, flowers, nectar and leaves. Feeding takes place in small groups from around dusk and like the Egyptian fruit bats they will circle a tree first – looking for predators or somewhere to land? At roost each individual will keep some distance to avoid confrontation and the inevitable fighting. These examples of the diversity must make bats one of the most distinctive and unequalled animals in the natural world today.

No feature would be complete without a mention of the vampires who have the distasteful habit of drinking blood. The three species of sanguivorous bats are found in both central and northern South America and its the common vampire *Desmodus rotundus* that takes mammalian blood. This athletic little 40g (1.4oz) bat with a 35-40cm (13-15ins) wingspan has unique ground dwelling skills to stalk prey. Often searching in groups strong hind limbs provide amazing jumping abilities. Once an animal is selected they can detect blood near to the skin surface and by using sharp hypodermic-like incisor teeth cut a tiny V shaped hole. As blood appears an enzyme called draculin in the bats saliva is introduced preventing clotting, this allows a small amount of blood to trickle which is then licked up. These bats must consume blood every 2 to 3 days or they will die and altruistic behaviours have been observed where individuals have regurgitated blood to others. A unique trait in the animal world. The victims are usually cattle or other domesticated animals and are completely unaware of what is going on. The end result is generally infection and disease. This bat has been known to take human blood but fortunately this is a rare event. There has been considerable research into the potential medical benefits from the clotting mechanisms.

Vampire Bat

Another successful bat that has adapted to a harsh environment is the pallid bat (*Antrozous pallidus*) of the western United States of America and central Mexico. This yellow and cream coloured 12cm (4.7ins) long animal survives in rocky arid deserts taking water only from their insect prey. Apart from good camouflage they have one other advantage when hunting and that is excellent hearing. This enables them to exploit the ground dwellers such as crickets and grasshoppers. Pallids are one of the few that are skilled in taking on scorpions. This has led to the bat being given the nickname - rambo bat. Other unusual facts about this particular bat are that twins are often born in the summer. There are strong social bonds between the females and their pups as many females have been observed apparently baby-sitting. It is also apparently common practice to share roosts with other bat species, clearly a bat that likes company.

The bat that everyone has heard of are the greater and lesser horseshoes both of which are sadly endangered and in trouble. When asked to name a bat these are the most likely to be mentioned, this is probably because they are better known than the others and have a distinctive name. Their genera name is *Rhinolophus* which means nose crest and is taken from the horse shoe shaped fold of skin on the nostrils, which is known as the nose leaf and through which the echolocating calls are directed. One of the principle reasons for the decline of the greater horseshoe is the loss of feeding grounds particularly around farmland and pasture. This reddish/brown coloured bat is only found in the south west of both England and Wales. Sadly this is a very rare and endangered bat suffering a huge 90% loss during the 20th century. They are also very sensitive to disturbance and pesticides, losing habitat also means losing insect prey. This species will emerge just after sunset to feed for perhaps an hour or so, then return to the roost and emerging again around dawn. As the cooler autumn weather approaches they may feed all night. This species often uses a perch in order to fly out from to capture insect prey such as moths as well as flying low to pick up beetles from the ground. Mating occurs during the autumn and occasionally as late as spring with maternity roosts being formed by June or July. These noisy colonies are known to get very hot so any clusters soon separate. The site selected is often a large building such as a church or a barn that receives good sunlight for warmth. Births will usually be at dusk and the timing is reliant on warm spring temperatures. A cold spring can have an adverse effect on numbers as individual females do not always breed each year. A single pup will be fed milk, by 5 weeks they can fly and hunt and are independent by 7 weeks. On the return of autumn, males will start to form territories around the maternity roosts. The females are not sexually mature until 3 years of age and the males not until the second or third year. From late September hibernation begins usually in disused mines, tunnels or cellars and the location may be some 50km (30 miles) from the maternity roost. In mild winter weather they may awake and hunt nearby. One fact that makes the greater horseshoe different from the other species is that they always choose a hibernation site that is warmer. It appears that the females tend to keep more fat reserves and stay put but the males may need to move from time to time. This species is also the longest lived of any European bat with records up to 30 years of age.

Elmstead Church

The brown coloured lesser horseshoe is about the size of a plum and is found only in south west England and in the west of both Wales and Ireland. There is a risk of extinction in the UK and the decline is due to the same reasons as the greater horseshoe. The lesser horseshoe is particularly sensitive to disturbance at the maternity roosts and this is when the work of the conservationists is important. These little bats will emerge at about dusk but often check the light first. They fly low feeding in and around the vegetation picking off prey quite often all night long, especially during the breeding season. They also seem to be the only UK species that will take small wasps. Mating takes place in the autumn with maternity roosts up and running by the following

April or May. Single pups are born from the middle of June to mid July and are independent and flying by 5 to 6 weeks. Most are mature enough to reproduce by their second year. Summer roosts will be in larger buildings, stables or other rural structures with plenty of roof space. The weather is particularly important as this might cause them to move if too hot or go into sleep-like torpor during a cold spell. Hibernation behaviours are similar to the greater horseshoe choosing somewhere warm with high humidity. Numbers of both species hibernating at any one time will vary but are rarely very large, individuals are often alone or in small groups.

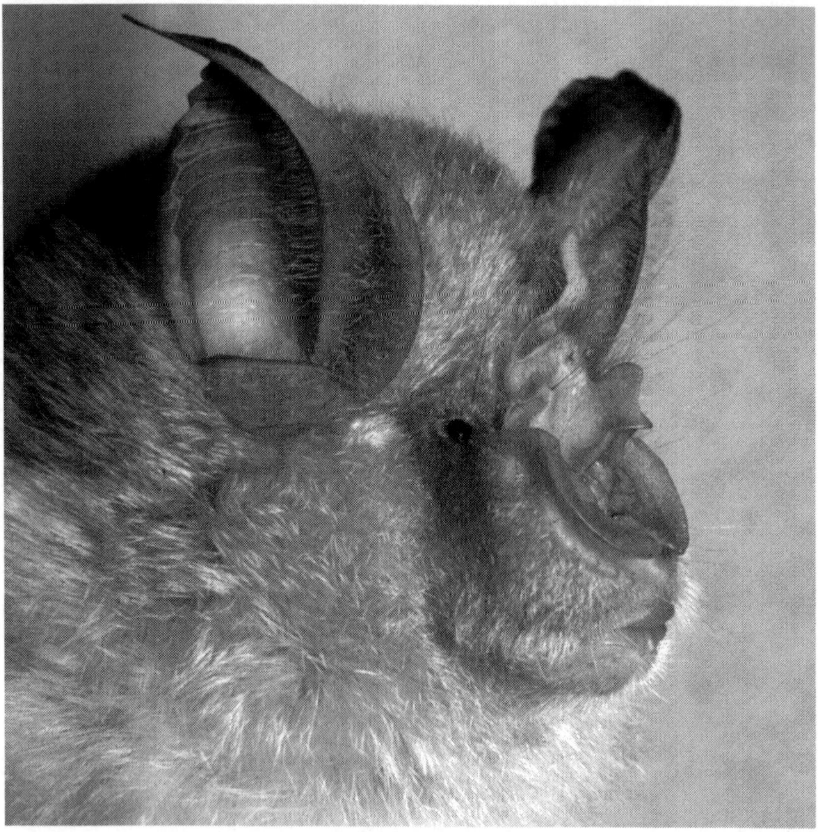

Greater Horseshoe Face

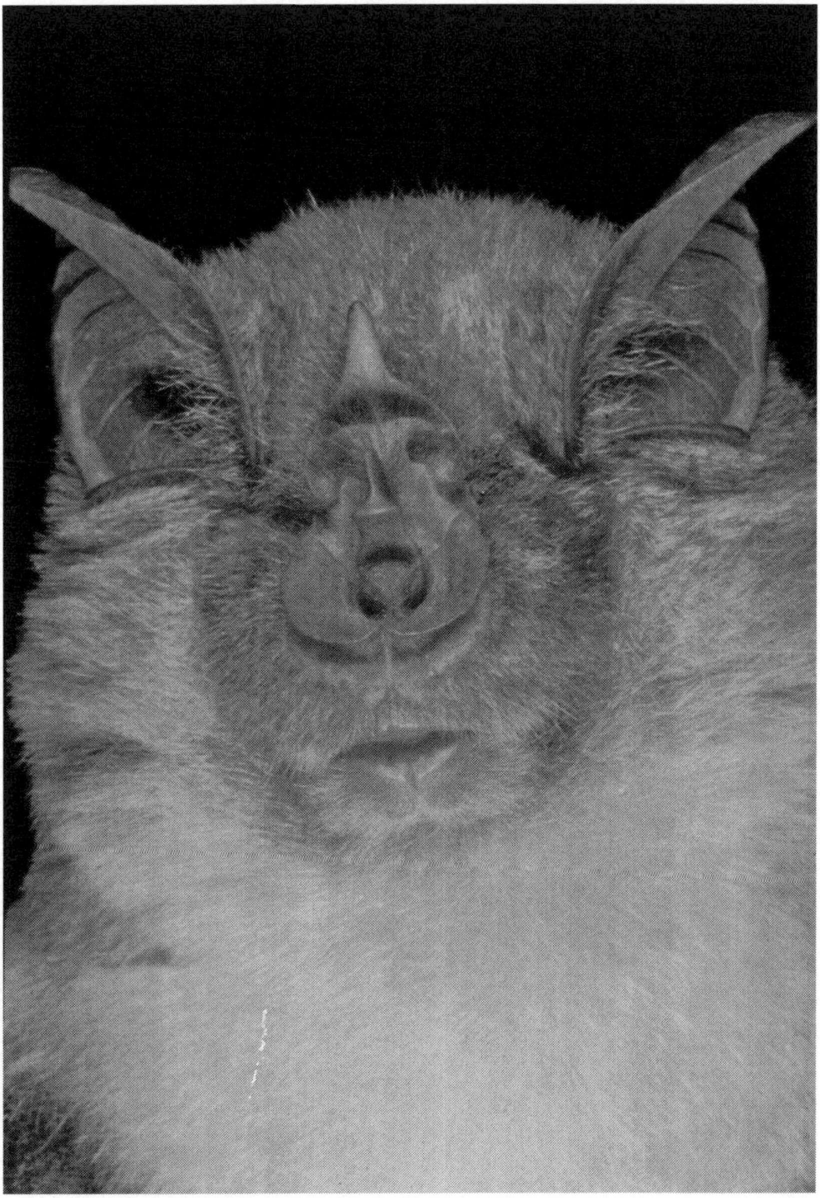

Greater Horseshoe Face-on and nose leaf detail

Greater Horseshoe hanging

Reproductive behaviours

Bats have evolved several strategies for breeding and clearly the survival of as many young as possible is the primary concern of the female. In the autumn male pipistrelles will mate with as many females as possible and try to keep a small harem within a defended territory. They give off a musky aroma and will engage in courtship flights. This particular species rely on a reproductive system known as delayed fertilisation where the egg remains infertile until ovulation and does not implant until a more appropriate time after hibernation. This ability is shared by many of the vespers. The growing fetus is dependent on the mother for survival who is able to provide nutrition, oxygen and remove waste. The tissues that cater for this are within the female uterus, or womb and are known as the placenta. Bats only have a short while to prepare for breeding and its important that the years young are fully developed and independent before the colder weather. In preparation for the forthcoming copulation the females will need sufficient food to survive hibernation and reproduce. The following spring is especially important for a breeding female, the need to find food in sufficient quantities to start building up strength and stamina is vital. The fetal development appears determined by the maternal body temperature which will be too low if there is a shortage of food. The development of young can be severely affected by temperature, so the subsequent maternity roost must be warm enough to enable the pregnant female prepare for the forthcoming birth. One of the benefits of a communal maternity roost is the provision of extra warmth within the roost area. Another is that a number of bats emerging and swarming at the same time might help avoid heavy predation. At this time the males will generally roost away from the females somewhere cooler and conserve energy. Meanwhile the gestating female may investigate other potential roosting sites and select another with better temperatures and humidity. Occasionally a site can become too hot and although bats can cope with extreme warmth, they might have to move deeper into the structure or perhaps elsewhere. Bats do not collect or use any kind of nesting material, once the nursery roost is chosen, they keep clear of draughts and simply hang up.

Woodland commuting route

Conservation

Accidentally or deliberately bats are disappearing mainly through habitat loss, pollution or extermination as some species are perceived as a threat or in many cases a lack of understanding or interest. Solutions can be found to many problems and good information is available through organisations such as the Bat Conservation Trust, local bat groups and other associated wildlife charities. Various groups around the world also promote protection and plan conservation initiatives through practical work in the field. Education and zoological collections also play a vital part in both roles.

It is a fact that these animals can be a nuisance and there are human health issues, but perhaps these matters should also be viewed in context. Bats have an essential and significant part to play in keeping down insect numbers. Equally important are the pollination of flowers and seed dispersal activities and the contribution to medical research, such as the vampire bats ability to clot blood, which may one day be of considerable relevance. Many are hunted for food and any unnecessary disturbance clearly does not help and due to little or no regulation many species are now endangered, some are extinct as a result. Many countries have also implemented legislation to protect and conserve these animals. It is very pleasing to be able to state that the UK is one of the principle leaders. In order to conserve it is good practice to gain knowledge about bats and one of the best ways to do this is by surveying, monitoring and maintaining records. I am indeed fortunate to have been able to take part in conservation work with the Wiltshire Bat Group. I have learnt a lot about planning objectives and the importance of identifying both practical and cost effective ways of completing such projects.

Part of this includes raising public awareness for this kind of programme over a period of years and there are many ways of doing this. The first priorities are to make sure that the correct licences are applied for and received from Natural England. Then to search out what records and information already exist. Once an area of good bat habitat is identified and there are no problems with access it is surveyed initially with detectors and ideally backed up with appropriate software which assists with subsequent analysis. This will help to define a specific territory of activity and will enable resources to be concentrated for initial surveys. These can be carried out on foot, by vehicle or a combination of both starting at around dusk as the bats emerge until the early hours. A similar survey can be carried out at around dawn when a roost has been located and the bats swarm just prior to entering and this can be an important step forward if this is a summer maternity roost. As and when individual species are identified the next challenge is to catch and sample flying bats. This allows conservationists to obtain information about sex, breeding condition, weight, forearm length and by closer examination the approximate age. Numbered rings can be attached to wings for recognition should individuals be caught again and the females are ringed on the left wing, the males the right. This also gives the opportunity to sample parasites and if necessary to obtain DNA for further research. Bats are usually captured by the use of mist nets which are suspended from poles at suitable sites such as foraging routes. Radio transmission devices can safely be attached to the bats body and this allows the individual(s) to be followed back to their feeding areas and roosts. The information can be invaluable in helping to decide what action is to be taken next to give further protection and how bats ecologically interact with the environment. This work is time consuming, but worth it and one of the best ways to help is to place bat boxes in the right places. It is also important to remember that all UK species are protected by law and a box must never be interfered with, even if it is believed to be unused.

Over time the loss of woodland throughout the world has reduced a lot of roosting sites, however artificial roosts can be a good alternative. Here in the UK it is believed that 11 species have been recorded roosting in boxes, some including the pipistrelle have bred and maintained maternity roosts. The latter should be large enough to allow a colony to bunch together thereby conserving heat. Bats may hibernate in a box although it is unlikey in very cold weather during the winter. Bat boxes can be purchased or built at reasonable prices and should be made with soft untreated wood. It is important that these are both rainproof and draught free. Rough sawn wood enables bats to climb about on the structure which should be at least 25mm (0.9") thick. The back board of the box should also be scored to help the bats grip and crawl. The entrance/exit has to be at the base of the box and should be 15 to 20mm (0.5" - 0.7") wide. The box can be held together with waterproof glue, nails or screws with an optional hinged watertight lid. Ideally a box should be attached to a non commercial mature tree with headless or domed nails made of iron and copper or aluminium alloy nails on conifers. A secure wire strap is also quite effective. The box has to be in a sheltered spot, between 2 and 4 metres (6.5 - 13.1ft) from the ground where it will be exposed to the sun and allow direct access, ideally with good woodland rides and perhaps marsh or nearby water. Such boxes can be useful in urban areas as well as rural due to there being suitable habitat in the towns and cities. No more than 3 boxes should be placed on any one tree and as each will be facing a different direction, the bats have a choice.

As already mentioned bats are protected by law and under no circumstances should there be any disturbance, but clearly they can be observed at dusk or dawn. It is equally important to bear in mind that during the summer it is possible that a box(es) may be occupied by a breeding group. Appropriate licences can be obtained and the best advise is available from the Bar Conservation Trust or a local bat group.

Bat Box (cross section)

Untreated wood from a sustainable source with the FSC logo
Must be watertight
Cut from 6" x 1" timber

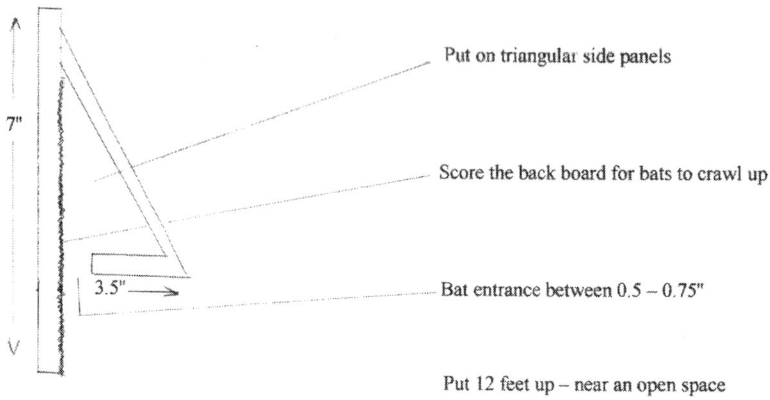

D. Chapman.

Lime kilns also provide good roosting opportunities

Bat Box similar to David Chapmans design

Conclusion

It appears that the bat is an adaptable and resourceful animal. From humble beginnings climbing about in the vegetation to the magnificent transformation which enabled descendants to fly and thrive.

These mammalian aviators have been an exceptional and unprecedented evolutionary success story.

Acknowledgements

Alana Ecology – Bat Detectors
Animal Diversity, University of Michigan
Arkive – Pipistrelle bats and Noctule bats
Aspinall, V. O'Reilly, M.- Introduction to Veterinary Anatomy and Physiology
Attenborough, D. - Life on Earth.
Bat Conservation Trust.
Bradley, S. - Ecology of Bat Reproduction
Brigg, B. King D. - The Bat Detective
Buczacki, S. - Fauna Britannica.
Dorit, R.L. Walker, F.W. Barnes, R.D. - Zoology
Drew, K. - Vampire Bat
Earth life - Blood
Ellis, M. - Nocturnals
Graham, G.L. - Bats of the World.
Hart - Davis, D. - Fauna Britannica
Heany, L.R. Heideman, P.D. Philippine Fruit bats : Endangered and Extinct
Hedenstrom, A. - Lifting the fog on bat flight - New Scientist
Hermanson, J.W. O'Shea, T.J. - *Antrozous pallidus* Mammalian Species
Hutson, T. - Bats
Hutson, T. - Bats and Climate Change
Kunz, T.H. Jones, D.P. - Mammalian Species
Longleat Safari Park
Lubee Bat Conservancy

Mammals Trust UK - Chiroptera
Michel, N. - The Biogeography of the Vampire Bat
Mulheison, M. Anderson, R. - *Desmodus rotundus*
Mulheisen, M. Berry, K. - Animal Diversity Web
Miller, D. *Antrozous pallidus*
Natural History Museum
Pederson, S. - Bathead
Pereira, M.J.R. *et al* - Status of the World's Smallest Mammal, the bumblebee bat (*Craseonycteris thonglongyai*) in Myanmar : Cambridge University Press
Preston, P.M. - The Natural History Collection - the evolution of Chiroptera
Racey, P.A. Swift, S.M.- Journal of Reproduction and Fertility
Rees, R. (Ed). - Philips Nature Encyclopedia
Richardson P. - Natural History Museum
Sender, T. Simon, M. - Journal of Animal Ecology
Simmons, N.B. Seymour, K.L. Habersetzer, J. Gunnell, G.F. - Primitive early Eocene bat from Wyoming and the evolution of flight and echolocation : Nature
Simons, N.B. Conway. T. Chiroptera - bats : The Tree of Life Web Project.
Simons, N.B. Conway, T. Microchiroptera - Echolocating bats : The Tree of Life Web Project.
Speakman, *et al* - Activity patterns of insectivorous bats and birds in northern Scandinavia during continuous midsummer daylight
Spedding, G. - Bat flight generates complex aerodynamic tracks : Science Daily
Teeling, E. - Bat evolution linked to warming
Thomas, S.P. Suthers, R.A. - The Physiology and Energetics of bat flight
Tudge, C. - New Scientist
University of Aberdeen
University of Bristol
Whitfield, P. - The Natural History of Evolution.
Wild About Britain - Northern Bat
Wiltshire Bat Group

Contacts and Credits

- Bat Conservation Trust, 15 Cloisters House, Battersea Park Road, London SW8 4BG
- Bat Helpline - 0845 -1300228.
- English Nature, Northminster House, Peterborough, PE1 1UA
- National Bat Monitoring Programme (help with surveys) c/o Bat Conservation Trust.
- Mammal Society, 3 The Carronades, New Road, Southampton, SO14 0AA
- Wildlife Trusts, The Kiln,Waterside, Mather Road, Newark, Nottinghamshire NG24 1WT

Photograph credits

Cover photo Egyptian fruit bat – A. Fairbairn

Bat Conservation Trust

Bat fossil – Bat Conservation Trust
Semi-albino soprano pipistrelle wing – Neville Thompson
Semi-albino soprano pipistrelle – Neville Thompson
Common pipistrelle – Hugh Clark
House roost access point (1) – Shirley Thompson
House roost access point (2) – Shirley Thompson
Noctule with juvenile – Hugh Clark
Tunnel (hibernation site) – Jules Agate
Union canal – Anne Youngman
Noctule hanging – John Altringham

Brown long-eared – Hugh Clark
Daubenton's bat – Hugh Clark
Daubenton's bat habitat – Anne Youngman
Barbastelle – J J Kaczanow
Bechstein's bat – Hugh Clark
Vampire bat – Shirley Thompson
Elmstead Church – Shirley Thompson
Greater horseshoe face – J J Kaczanow
Greater horseshoe face-on – J J Kaczanow
Greater horseshoe hanging – J J Kaczanow
Woodland commuting route – Bob Cornes
Lime kilns – Anne Youngman
Bat box – J J Kaczanow

Thanks to David Chapman for the bat box design
Bat wing drawing by the author